CW01562260

My name is Nick Foster, I am t
Victor Foster (Jack) who in 200
memories of the second world war. Unfortunately,
most of his memories were made behind German
barbed wire.

Born in London in 1920 but shortly after moved to
Curry Rivel, Somerset. His formative years in the
sleepy agricultural west country village did little to
prepare him for life in his 20's.

The Grandad that I knew through my childhood was
kind, loving and renowned for his sense of humour by
all that knew him.

He never meant for this book to be a published, but
even the people who read his "draft" yet never had
the privilege of meeting him insisted that there is an
audience out there who would appreciate it.

"The human spirit is stronger than anything that can happen to it."

–George C. Scott

Sauerkraut & Boiled Potatoes

My story begins in April 1939 When I enlisted in the R.A.F. for a period of six years, to be trained as a wireless operator. I went to west Drayton to sign on the dotted line, and having done so, was immediately checked for a haircut, together with most of the other recruits.

A barber's shop in any high Street would contain mirrors, and you would be asked how you would like it cut, but in this establishment, not a mirror to be seen, and they certainly did not enquire how you wanted it cut.

The next day we travelled to Cordington, near Bedford. There were two very large hangars here which had housed two airships, the R100 and R101. The Latter crashed in Northern France, killing several of the crew. We came here to do our initial training and be kitted out in uniforms, etc. I enjoyed this very much; cross-country running, sports, marching on the parade ground with a brass band playing marches; as a small boy, I played the cornet in the village band, and have enjoyed this type of music ever since.

When we passed out, the flight sergeant said we were a seedy Looking bunch before we started and now look at yourselves, bolt upright, (which in my case was only Five feet six inches!!).

The food was very good. During our main meal, an Officer came around saying in a loud voice, "Any complaints? It would have taken a brave airman to have stood up and said Yes, Sir

The Sunday morning church parade in the camp Church was compulsory. One airman had forgotten to take his hat off. A sergeant bawled across the Church, Take your hat off in the house of God you silly bugger...

I walked into the town of Bedford and had my photo taken in uniform. Our next move was to the Wireless Training School, near Yatesbury in Wiltshire, not far from Calne. I recently went back there with my family, to where the camp had been, now just a field of barley and a large stone where the guard room had been, with information carved into the stone. we also paid a visit to the Public House which I used to visit on saturday nights, together with the other airmen. The landlady produced a book which had been signed by other returning airmen over the years, so I duly signed, and told her it was sixty-seven years ago that I last set foot in here

I spoke to a local man in the bar and mentioned that we were going to see the famous Silbury Hill, a manmade hill where the earth had been taken from the surrounding area thousands of years ago. He said, "No, that is not exactly true, it was where the local council workmen used to scrape their shovels off when leaving work!"

Most of our time was spent in the classroom learning to send and receive the Morse code, and the theory of radio. I missed the exercise and marching to a brass band. We all listened on the radio to Neville

Chamberlain declaring war on Germany. Just a few days later, a line of London double-decker buses came along, travelling west, full of children, who I felt sorry for because they were so young.

It became very cold in November. Pipes became frozen solid, so we were sent home for a few days. In December, our lessons came to an end. We then had a short flight in an aircraft, fitted with a transmitter, and contacted base.

In December, about fifty of us were detailed to be sent to France with the B.E.F. to co-operate with spotter planes by radio. This was a system used in the 1914-18 war, and completely unsuited to modern warfare, as we were soon to find out. Over the Christmas period, we were sent home on embarkation leave, and to report back to Uxbridge R.A.F. station near London. I said my goodbyes to my parents and my grandfather, and my two brothers.

From Uxbridge we travelled by coach to Southampton and sailed overnight to Cherbourg, then by train to Amiens. We then marched a couple of miles to a small airfield with grass runways and a hangar

We were billeted in buildings which had beds mounted on trestles to clear the floor. These were pushed over every night by the returning drunks. One evening when everyone was in bed and the lights had been turned out, a man from the canteen brought back one airman who had had too much to drink, and he was seeing him safely back. However, when the canteen chap tried to leave, the airman would yell out "Don't leave me Dad, don't leave me". After a little of this, the whole barrack was advising Dad to "F* off, Dad."

The small service bus, which catered for the locals to get to Amiens, started to become full of airmen, and Locals were very often having to stand, much to their annoyance. I didn't help on one occasion, when I was the Last on it was a sliding door operated by the driver. On reaching Amiens, he yanked the door back, I fell out backwards onto the pavement with a Frenchwoman on top of me. A great cheer went up from the lads in the bus. She did not think it was funny and threatened me with her finger.

While playing table tennis in the canteen one evening, we lost the ball behind the spare table. I pulled it back to see where the ball had gone, my hand slipped off and went through the window, cutting my wrist open right to the tendons. I was taken to a hospital in, Amiens, stayed for a few days, then back to camp.

Not long after, we had to pair off and were then issued with a Radio Receiver. Then Army units appeared, and we all went our different ways. I have no idea where we went from day to day, until we ended up in front of the Maginot Line in the area of Metz. The small village was empty of civilians. My mate, whose name was George, and myself found ourselves a house with some comfortable mattresses, and settled in, thankful to be in one spot for a while.

The R.A. battery we were attached to consisted of all ex-servicemen who had seen service in India. In the cookhouse we were hearing Indian words for some of the food, Pozzy was jam, Burgoo was porridge, etc.

The Artillery consisted of twenty-five pounder field guns. The French had been sending over a couple of shells per day, and jerry would send two back. Then the Brits moved in and fired a dozen or so. This had the effect of stirring up a hornet's nest, so they stopped doing that or else someone was going to get hurt. After leaving Amiens, we were not going to see another R.A.F. Officer or airman.

One day, we volunteered to help collect some ammo from a wood, as we were bored. The road we travelled along was shielded from the east by hessian so that Jerry could not see what was passing along it. Then one day, without any warning, the gunners hitched up the guns to the tractors and away. We just managed to scramble on board an ammunition Lorry with kit and receiver. We had no idea why the hurry but later we soon knew the blitz had begun up in the north.

Our first position was on a hillside with good cover for the guns, then put down a barrage in the evening, which was Quite a sight, with the flashes from the guns and the noise was terrific.

Next morning, a swarm of Stukas came over and dive bombed a French battery which was next door to us. Later that day we were asked to collect their dinner from some woods to the rear. When we found it, it had been hit by shell, so no hot food but tinned meat; the Gunners were none too pleased. Some heavy shelling followed, and later that day the order was

7

given to retreat. George and I made sure of getting on a tractor and we went back about eight miles passing some French cavalry. The horses were exhausted, and some riders were walking beside them.

When the guns were set up, a telephone wire was taken forward of the position for a long way. This was an observation post for the guns. We listened to the report coming back. The range was gradually reducing until the order came to move. I was impressed with the speed they hitched up the guns to the tractors. George and I made sure we got a seat.

Then another seven or eight miles to the next position; this was an orchard with a large farmhouse close by. A Jerry spotter plane came over flying very low. An infantry soldier took a shot with a Bren gun on a tripod, but no luck.

The farmer and family had probably left the day before, as the cows were running around bellowing and the milk was coming out of their teats. I think they were in pain. The poor farmer must have been worried sick. That evening, we were informed that we should be walking to the coast to be taken off by boats. The guns were spiked. I think that entailed putting a shell in the wrong way around - am not sure about that.

We set out walking, later passing lines of trucks with engines ticking over, the oil plugs had been taken out and they would eventually seize up. Hand grenades were scattered everywhere. It was dark when we reached St Valery, a small harbour surrounded by hills. A few houses were on fire. we stayed on the hill overlooking the town. It started to rain hard, so I covered my head with a ground sheet, rather than sit on it. By the next morning, I was fairly dry. No sign of any boats standing off the harbour

Machine guns were firing from the west bank, so it seemed that we were surrounded. A bugle sounded down in the town a soldier said that was the cease fire. An Officer came around ordering everyone to destroy rifles. They were throwing away the bolts. George and attacked the radio with gusto!!

A couple of shells came over to remind us they were around, then we spotted two tanks approaching. One stopped close by, and a big German got out waving his pistol.

Prisoners of War

THE following is the latest list of R.A.F. prisoners in enemy hands. Received from German sources.

P/O. Hanlon, Ottawa. Sqn. Ldr Kennedy, Cape-town, Sgt. Remnant, Acton, W.3 (all three shot down near Lenwig, Denmark, or Lenvik, Norway). Flt. Lt., H. J. Rowe, Shepperton, Middx.; A/C.1 J. A. Webster, Liverpool; Sgt. C. H Loane, Sunderland; Sgt. J. A. Lucke, Weston, Middx.; A/C.1 R. R. Shuttleworth, Ilford; P/O. Drinney, address not known (wounded); P/O. C. C. Jackson, Croydon; A/C.2 J. V. Foster, Taunton, Somerset; A/C.2 G. Snowball. New Silksworth; Sgt. W. H. Eden, Winnipeg; Sgt. C. Webb (West?), Much

Then began an horrendous forced march to Holland that evening. After being herded into a field like animals, they started throwing loaves of bread over - there was a mad rush to get one; as hungry as I was, I could not bring myself to take part in this degrading spectacle, so I went hungry.

The Summer of 1940 was very hot. I had a water bottle which I found useful. Passing through villages or towns, the French and Belgian women were bringing out buckets of water, which the kindly Germans promptly kicked over. They were on top of the world and being issued with food was out of the question. Frenchwomen would have bread hidden behind their backs and if you were lucky you would get some, which happened for me one day. I always used my R.A.F. satchel for a pillow, so this long French loaf I put under the satchel, with my water bottle close by. The next morning, when I awoke, both ends had been cut off the loaf and my water bottle had taken a walk. I had not seen George for several days and had been walking with a soldier who never had a bottle. He said, "Don't worry, I will get another". When being hounded out of this field, he calmly lifted a bottle from the man in front.

A Frenchwoman, who had upset a Jerry Officer, was being beaten by him with a large stick. On going through town now, the soldiers were being ordered to fix bayonets to keep civilians from feeding P.O.W's.

On reaching the Eastern end of Belgium, I began to feel really ill. My soldier friend told me later that we had been loaded onto trucks (railway) and finished up beside a large canal. I cannot remember anything of this journey, just being taken aboard a large motorised barge when I came to my senses. Then followed a journey up this large waterway. Dutch people on the bank were shouting "You will come back, Tommy"

I remember seeing a large sign on the eastern side which was Delft. Chaps were suffering problems with their stomachs. Their mates would hold their hands while they did it over the sides. At the end of this journey, we were loaded into cattle trucks and arrived in Essen, Germany, into a large park. A queue formed hopefully to be issued with some grub. When Jerry officer noticed my uniform to be different. I was taken to a building wherein were several high-ranking British Officers, one of whom gave me a cigarette.

Later that day, I was put on a passenger train together with three or four other airmen, but no sign of George, who I never saw again. We were on our way to a Dulag Luft, near Frankfurt; this served as our interrogation Lager, where POW's were asked questions about their activities before capture, etc. You are only allowed to give your name, rank and service number - a standing joke amongst aircrew was that one was asked how his Auntie Mabel was keeping these days?

One night was spent here, then on a passenger train to Barth, which was on the Baltic coast. We passed through Berlin; the journey seemed endless, but thankfully we were not in cattle trucks.

We walked to this Lager from Barth; it was named Stalag Luft 1. On entering, I saw what appeared at first glance to be monkeys in a zoo, clinging to the barbed wire and shouting. They had recently their heads shaved because of an outbreak of typhus which can only be caused by lice.

This turned out to be POWs asking if they knew anyone from such and such a squadron. I was allocated a bunk in a room holding sixteen in two tiered wooden beds, with a straw mattress laid on boards, slotted into the sides.

F32 Stalag Luft 1

We were given an enamel bowl to eat out of. The members of this room had all been shot down over France and Germany; we were together in this room for almost two years. I can remember them individually to this very day, some of whom stand out in my memory.

One earned himself the nickname Bing because he was always singing, which sometimes became a bit much: another seemed to suffer with nerves; he had a permanent blink. When Red cross parcels began arriving in 1941, they contained cigarettes, which this chap would very soon smoke. He would then ask for a 'drag'; at first we would give it to him, but then it was difficult to get it back. So then we would hold the cigarette to his lips. He was called Blinker, which sounds cruel, but it wasn't really. He then said he would do some washing for cigarettes, but he ran of customers because the finished product was none too special. Then another chap was always breaking wind. He would then say "Manners have long been our boast"

Every part of the British Isles had a representative in this room. On Christmas Day 1940, we were living solely on German rations. I know exactly what we had for dinner - a two inch square of pork, boiled potatoes in their jackets and sauerkraut, which was pickled cabbage of a kind, something you would only eat if you were hungry, and that, Ladies and Gentlemen was it, not forgetting the ersatz coffee, reputably made from acorns and nothing like coffee in taste. No cigarettes. I was very depressed that day, wondering if my parents had had any news of me.

The winters here were cold, temperatures dropping to minus 20 degrees at night, but the barracks were insulated, so it didn't get too cold inside. A chap from another room started shouting to the guard in the tower, using abusive German. A small crowd gathered to watch; that is until the guard swivelled his machine gun around to point at this chap, who had earned himself the name Mad Stacey' because, when writing home on the special form, he would write that the Germans were bastards, etc. The censor would read this, and he would be sent for, to spend some days in the Cooler', a name given to a block of cells overlooking the compound. Then when we were counted, morning and evening, he would pull himself up to the iron grill and scream.

I am standing on the right-hand side and needing a haircut - Picture taken winter 1941/42.

We had just enough space to kick a football around. One chap in particular that I remember took little short steps, and he was called 'Twinkle Toes'. He had been shot down flying a Blenheim Bomber in 1939. It was said that his wife was expecting at the time. I shall be mentioning him again later in my story.

The toilets were primitive, consisting of a long concrete pit with wooden seats constructed over the top. It was the breeding ground for flies in the summer. When it was full, a man driving a horse and cart, with a large tank fixed, would put a pipe into the pit then pump some petrol vapour into a turret and ignite it. This caused an explosion causing a vacuum in the tank and sucking the effluent up. The driver had been a Pow in World war 1 and spoke a little English. He seemed to have had one over the eight and gave me some cigarettes. German cigarettes were mostly oval in shape, except for one brand called 'Juno'. On the packet was a slogan, 'Es gud und grund, ist juno Rund' roughly translated as 'Junos are good and tasty when round'

An interpreter, Herr Becker, was a kindly German. Mr Barraclough in the comedy series in Slade prison always reminds me of him. He came around every morning, asking if there were any zick'? one of our chaps said yes, he was "zick of this f***ing place".

Two chaps attempted an escape through the wire. One was shot dead. He was laid out in a small room which served as a church, and we lined the route from here to the gate when he was taken out to be buried. I have pictures of this from a contact with an amateur radio member living near Barth who has sent me the photos and who has visited the site of the former Stalag Luft 1, where a stone has been erected to mark the spot.

About a dozen of us were sent out to work near Barth, picking out cobblestones from a ditch alongside a concrete road. we messed about, picking up one stone and then stopping for a chat. A couple of German workmen arrived on their bikes in the morning, greeting the guards with a small salute and a Heil Hitler. We would then say Heil Churchill. We were not working hard enough for the German foreman, so he put a German in the ditch to set the pace, so we would then drop every other one, so at the end of the week we got the sack. Then they sent us to a storage building for sacks of grain, and that did not last for long.

On walking into the town of Barth I noticed in one street there were wing mirrors attached to the windows, so the residents could watch who was coming down the street. We used to make faces when passing!!

The winter became very cold. A lot of snow fell and drifted, blocking the road into the camp, so we were sent out to clear it. I think it snowed most winters up here because they used horse drawn sledges. I also saw two oxen pulling a plough, and storks nesting on a derelict chimney.

Jerry tried showing some propaganda film in the dining hall. We would not stop laughing all through the film, so that put paid to that. Germans do not like to be laughed at.

Red cross parcels began arriving sometime in 1941, and life began again. it was wonderful real tea and butter, tins of meat, cigarettes, etc, books to read (you put your name on the waiting list), packs of playing cards, Monopoly, Ludo. I learnt to play Bridge, a league was formed, and you went along to another barrack to play. It became the custom to make tea for the visiting team, but tea was precious, and after the first brew, the leaves were dried, then used again which meant they had to be boiled to get any colour.

This became known as seconds' and this is what you would get when playing away. They would take a sip and say, "This is bloody seconds!!"

The second Christmas Day, 1941, was entirely different to the first. My parents had received a letter from me, and we had enough to eat, cigarettes to smoke, tea, etc. The end of the war seemed years away. Jerry was racing through Russia, and as a POW you have no idea how long you will be behind barbed wire. This is one of the hardest things to overcome, a criminal is given a sentence, and knows he will be free at the end of it.

In April 1942, we were moved to Stalag Luft 3. This one was much better in terms of room to move outside the barracks, room enough for a full-size football pitch, though the toilets were still primitive. We travelled by the luxurious cattle trucks; I cannot remember how Long this took, certainly two days or more. We were now in Poland, near the German border. Sagan was the name of the small town close by.

The barracks were not divided up into rooms, with, I would say, about 100 men to each barrack. There was a small room at the end of which contained a stove. A large barrack was kept for recreation where stage plays were acted. Red cross parcels kept on arriving and life was bearable. We kept our room in Stalag 1 together, as we knew each other's mothers' maiden names!!

One of our members of that room took to staying on his bed and reading the Bible all day Long. We did not realise at the time that he was seriously depressed and wrote on the side of his bed a religious slogan. He went outside to the toilets and tried to end it. Fortunately, he was found in time and was eventually repatriated to England.

If you opened a tin of meat, it had to be eaten quickly so we formed 'combines', consisting of five or six men who would pool certain items in the parcel, so that a tin, once opened, would be eaten up. On Christmas Day 1942, a member of the combine that I was in made a trifle in a washing up bowl. I didn't enjoy this because there was a tide mark inside the bowl.

We began to receive the BBC news courtesy of an airman who was a genius at making radio set condensers made up from silver paper from cigarette tins and bulbs from guards who were bribed with cigarettes. The news was taken down in shorthand and secretly taken around each barrack and read out. This raised the morale tremendously especially when Churchill made one of his wonderful speeches

The toilets were a breeding ground for flies in the summer; which invaded the barracks and were a menace. To pass the time of day, a craze started which entailed catching a large fly, tying cotton to its legs, then making a drogue from cigarette paper and tying it to the cotton. we would then climb up to the top bunk and let it go. It would fly at half speed amidst roars of Laughter, then they would see who could get one to fly the furthest. A chap named Grimson was always making escape attempts. He spoke German, and on this occasion, he had made a Ladder, dressed up in overalls, and, carrying a so-called electrician's kit, he approached the warning wire which ran around the camp some yards from the main wire. In this case notice had been erected which said Do not touch warning wire, or it will be shot". Grimson shouted to the guard in the box that he had come to repair a searchlight next to the guard Tower. The Guard gave him permission to cross. He climbed up the ladder and made out he was working on this light. He then dropped some pliers, got down the wire on the outside and explained to the Guard that he needed to get some spares. He then walked into the wood which surrounded the Stalag on three sides and he was away. When we went on parade that evening, the Ladder was still there, chaps were digging one another in the ribs and saying "Grimson's gone again". That man did not have any nerves, he did not survive the war.

When being counted, it often took ages. Germans cannot count. It was during one of these long waits that one chap got talking to a guard who was to the rear of us, while his mate stuck a lit cigarette into the top of his rifle. He was then walking up and down with the cigarette merrily smoking away with a good draught up the barrel. I expect the guard wondered why everyone was smiling at him. The chap from our room in, Stalag 1, who was always breaking wind used to reserve his best for when we were lined up together; this caused some amusement.

In the evenings before lock up, it became customary to walk around the perimeter to talk about the day's happenings. Herr Becker came to Stalag 3. I often wonder what became of him when the war ended.

Around this time, someone made a crochet needle from an old tooth brush handle, then unthreaded some old socks and made himself a woolly hat. How on earth did this man know how to crochet? This caught on Like wildfire: very soon socks were being dismantled and made into some queer looking hats, which were proudly worn in the evenings on the walk before lock up.

One of my mates started to make a model stage coach, so I became involved and collected some silver paper, which I melted down and poured into a mould I had made from German soap, in the shape of a wheel. It turned out fine. We paid a German in cigarettes take a photo of the completed coach, which I still have.

To boil water with the least amount of fuel, we made a "blower" from tins from the parcels. It consisted of a fan which was geared up to blow very fast. It was mobile, and some specimens were a work of art. It became very competitive to make the best. I was no good at this, but I could crochet.

We would sometimes be paid a visit from a Jerry sergeant who spoke fluent English with an American Accent. He was only looking for signs of a tunnel or radio set or whatever his beady eyes could pick up. We all knew his game, so nothing was ever given away. His name was Glemnitz.

Some good plays were acted out in the recreation building, a pianist gave us some wonderful music to listen to we were paid a visit one day by the Gestapo, wearing breeches and trilby hat with a feather sticking out. The barracks were mounted on poles, so that Jerry could see if any tunnels were being made. A Gestapo man was passing an open window when a hand shot out and grabbed his hat.

Football was played on a full-sized pitch. I once made up the number in a rugby league game, never having played this game before. I decided after the game was over that it was my last time.

In May 1943, we left Stalag Luft 3 in luxurious cattle trucks, for Stalag Luft 4 in East Prussia. On entering the camp, the workmen, who had been patching up the barracks had left off-cuts of wood lying around. These were very soon gathered up for future brews with the blowers, As I have said, the original occupants of the room in Stalag Luft 1 still kept together when moved. We found a corner and settled in.

We were not far from the Lithuanian border. The radio travelled safely and Red Cross parcels found us. That summer, we had lots of sunshine; chaps were sunbathing, some in the nude. The commandant was proudly showing his wife around from the outside, chaps stood up to watch, so she got a free view. Don't look now, Ethel!!

American POWs were now arriving in the next compound. Shots were fired because they were ignoring the sign, "Do not touch or it will be shot" During this Summer we held a Fete on the football space: one stall had a notice fixed to a blanket, "come and see the man lying on a bed of nails. Price 2 cigarettes". I had 2 cigarettes worth, and was carefully conducted into the inner sanctum of blankets to see a man with his shirt off lying on some bed boards which were strewn with loose assorted nails.

Another stall advertised, "come and see the camels This was empty camel cigarette packets obtained from the Yanks. There were also several 'Swap Shops' which contained items for sale, or you could swap items over, not unlike Pawn Shops in England. The currency here was cigarettes.

Polish members of the R.A.F. were very clever making items from wood or anything which was to hand. One in particular I remember, was a figure of a cross inside a bottle, with a wooden stopper which stretched down to the neck. He would challenge anyone to take the stopper out, which we could not do. He would then turn his back and take it out in seconds. Another made a glider which he got into the air by racing across the compound; it would soar over the camp, then one time it soared out of the camp, but Jerry would not give it back; 'charming'. Another made rings from horse hair, which they obtained from horses delivering goods to the cookhouse, by snipping it from their tails. A German Jew who was in the R.A.F. gave lessons to learn the language. I started but gave it up. Two chaps were making cartoons which were posted up on the notice board. Some of them were brilliant, they were published in a book after the war. I still have the copy I obtained, it is well worn.

Talks were given by chaps who could talk the hind leg off a donkey, so the cartoonists made one, showing the notice board with the following 'My Life in wales' by G.A. Price, 'Scotland, my Scotland' by G.A. Price, 'My Irish Home' by G.A. Price, etc.

Tunnels were being made from the toilet block close to the main wire. Jerry thought of a cunning plan by bringing in a diesel roller which they thought would collapse any being built. Spectators gathered to watch this, and when the front roller sank into one, they could not, at first, get it out. it would get to the rim and fall back in. Chaps were throwing their crochet hats into the air and cheering. Eventually, they managed and brought the roller across the compound which was very sandy. They got stuck, so they found some planks which they ran the roller on to, then picking up the two from the rear to place in front. Before they could pick them up, however, chaps were running away with them. A good time was had by all until the guards had been sent for, including Alsatian dogs. There was a mad scramble to get back to the barracks.

A lorry was sent to collect so many bed boards from each bed, because they were being used to shore up the tunnels, out as fast as they loaded them, they were taken back, that is until a jerry guard arrived complete with Tommy Gun. He stood on top of these boards inviting anyone to help themselves, but there were no takers!!

With the increasing numbers of night time air raids taking place, there were lots more air crew POWs arriving in this camp. A small number were taken to each barrack, wherever jerry could push in more two-tiered bunks. In our barrack, about two more were found room. One of my mates said one of them had an accent similar to my own, why didn't I talk to him. I was not interested, then this chap came to see me and his first words were, "What be thy name then?" it turned out that he knew my younger brother, and had been in the village just a few weeks earlier.

Prisoners could receive a personal parcel from home containing clothes, very few arrived. Whenever they did, the lucky recipient would open it on the table, prisoners would gather round to watch, and also take part by lifting up a new shirt or pants and admiring them. It was something like kids opening their presents on Christmas day

When newly captured airmen arrived in a barrack, they would be interrogated by the old timers; they were always asked if they had a girlfriend. If they did, then they were advised to forget her, because he would very soon get a "Dear John" letter. Some of them would be indignant and say perhaps that they had been friends for a very long time. Prisoners would laugh and say that the letter would probably begin, "I will not be writing any more, as I love a soldier".

On one journey in the cattle trucks, because of an attempted escape by prisoners through the floor, a guard rode in each truck separated by a wire enclosure with the doors partly open and a lantern in the roof. There was no room to lie outstretched, so we tried sleeping with heads on knees. A chap opposite me had his kit attached to a nail above his head. He was asleep and knocking his head on the side of the truck with the motion, when his kit fell on his head.

The lantern was rocking backwards and forwards. We were flat out on the square wheels, it seemed to me at that moment so unreal, that I started to laugh. Very soon the whole truck was bursting, to make matters worse I knew they had no idea what they were laughing at.

When we received news of the invasion, the nightly walk around the perimeter was crowded. Chaps excitedly talking about it and praying that we would not be driven off. Then two days later when chaps were lying on their beds, reading or carving a bit of wood, the barrack room door burst open, and a chap walked quickly down the gangway between the beds shouting out "They're off, they're off", implying that our troops had been driven off, then he paused on going out the door the other end, and said they have started!!! He was surely the future father of Jeremy Beadle. It was a good job he didn't hang about, giving people heart attacks like that.

The Winter of 1943/1944 was cold, the camp had become so full that POWs were sleeping in tents. On christmas Day 1943, we had made some wine from the prunes in the Red cross parcels, Jerry jam ration, yeast from a guard and whatever else that might be suitable. That evening, the doors would not be locked and you could visit each block provided you did not go beyond the so-called red lines, as laid down by Jerry.

The galvanised bucket that our brew had been made in came up like new. It was poison and very intoxicating. I could think of better ways of spending Christmas.

The Russians had turned the tide, and were now threatening Poland. We had 24 hours to pack our belongings, so we started to off-Load some of our kit. The more recent POWs were picking up what they required from what we were dumping. The next day we were lined up and marched off at a brisk pace, with shouts of "Los Los Schnell". On arriving at a railway siding, we saw our beloved cattle trucks waiting for us. I watched a chap who was carrying too much kit attached to his back, and took the weight off by resting it on a window sill of a bungalow. A guard booted it off spinning the chap around. He was immediately called a square headed German bastard.

This particular train journey lasted for what seemed days. At this particular stage of the war, air raids were regular. Yanks were coming over on daylight raids. Trains would stay in sidings by day, and then when it became dark, they would go like the clappers, which seemed to happen to us. On one occasion when parked, a member of the truck had dysentery and asked the guard who was standing by the truck, if he could get down and relieve himself. The guard said "No", so this chap said he would have to do it in the truck. He was voted down 100-1, so he then begged the guard to rethink, which he did reluctantly. He had just got his trousers down when a whistle sounded, and the trucks started moving. The guard panicked and tried to get this chap back into the truck. It was a false alarm, thankfully. it caused some laughter in the truck which, I am sure, remains in their memories.

We asked the guard if he could ask the train driver for some hot water to make tea. It came back a brown colour before the tea was added.

Eventually we arrived at a Polish town called Thorn. We walked through a side street which seemed deserted. On going into this lager, we passed between compounds wherein were what might have been Russians. We threw some cigarettes over and in the rush they were falling over with weakness. The rooms here were so packed together with bunks, it was not easy to get up into the top bunk. Heath

Robinson would have been proud of the toilets had he made them.

We arrived here on 16th July 1944, and Left on 10th August 1944. while here, an attempt was made on Hitler's life. It was rumoured that an R.A.F. Polish airman had been speaking to a relative through the wire.

Our next move was to take us to Falling Bostel in Germany. This was going to be our last Stalag. The barracks were similar to all the previous ones, with the usual two-tiered bunks and straw mattresses, the toilet block was situated in the middle of the compound a concrete pit with wooden seats above it. In this Stalag, we had a thirty-six seater, with a bar running down the middle, so men were sitting back to back, pure luxury! Chaps would sit and talk about the progress of the war, when you got back to the barrack you would mention something you had heard, this would immediately be condemned as being 'shit house gen'. We had books in the library which had been read a dozen times by the same person.

We arrived in this Stalag on 12th August 1944. We began to hear our bombers passing over during the night. On a morning counting parade, the Commandant announced German POWs in North Africa had to sleep on the sand, so we were going to have our mattresses taken away. The next day, a lorry arrived with several men and began doing just that. They were stored in a barrack within the compound and locked up. With Winter approaching this was not funny.

Red Cross parcels had dried up because of transport problems, so we were back on German rations, which were being cut regularly we had no heating or lights after dark.

Amongst several thousand men, you always get someone who stands out as being different. That man was in our barrack. He would get up in the morning and go out naked to the cold water tap and splash about, while we were shivering in our beds. He must have had a skin like a rhino. His hair was shaped with a one inch strip down the middle of his head, about two or three inches long, so you could safely say that he was different.

We began dreaming almost every night about food. I was always seeing large lumps of suet pudding, swimming in treacle; others would see perhaps bacon, eggs and sausages.

It was becoming a hard winter; our ribs were becoming visible, and if we sat up in bed too quickly we would become giddy. I began to worry that we could not exist on this meagre ration. If we became ill, we had not the strength to fight it.

It was arranged that a chap who had a story to tell would come into the barracks before lock up, with his blanket and stand up and talk in the dark for some time. One such man I remember was an Australian who had been opal digging. They claimed a site and began digging, living on the spot. Another was a

Canadian who bailed out over a town. His chute became entangled around the top of a factory chimney. The next day, a German, climbed the iron ladder, threw him a rope, he released his chute and swung down to the ladder. Another had been in the Police Force in London. This all helped to keep up morale.

Christmas Day was 1940 all over again, except that we could see the end of the war was not far off. My parents knew that I was alive and kicking. One day, a cry went up that we were getting the mattresses back, so there was a mad rush to the barrack containing them. There was a mad scramble going on, some trying to get in the one door, and chaps already in trying to get out, dust everywhere. The barracks soon became empty, the locksmith had done a good job, everyone went to bed early that night, amidst cries of "ooh this is bloody Lovely', but not for long. The next morning, a lorry collecting mattresses appeared. Jerry was losing the war and it was hurting.

Around January, February time, America was bombing by day. Some passed over the Stalag, flying in perfect formation a wonderful sight for us. We began cheering like mad, throwing the crochet hats into the air. This became too much for Jerry and guards were sent in to drive us back into the barracks. We were very pleased to think that had got under their skin.

At some time in March, we were informed that next day we would be leaving the Stalag. It turned out that we were lined up with what kit we could carry given a loaf of bread, no margarine, and marched out going eastwards. We did not cover many miles per day, as we were too weak to walk very fast. At night we slept mostly in farmyards. Some chaps ate their Loaf of bread in next to no time, I expect Blinker ate his the same day! I made mine last as long as possible; Jerry never fed us again. We would raid potato dumps, bordering the roads, The guards were old men who had seen service in World war 1. One night we slept in a large barn containing bales of straw; that was lovely.

Another occasion, we found some leeks growing in a farmer's garden. we started pulling them up, until fired on by a guard, probably over our heads.

We came to the River Elbe, which was very wide at this point. A large bridge spanned the river with a small village nestling on the Eastern bank. We had to wait some time before crossing, to let Jerry tanks over going west. Soldiers were riding on top taking up every available space. About two days Later, we were informed that a convoy of Lorries had left Switzerland with Red cross parcels looking for POWs who were being marched East. We were going to get one parcel between two, and would collect them from the next village we came to. This was marvellous news, and we paired up to collect, then marched some two miles and stopped alongside the road to open them. The chap I paired with, who I did not know, said he hoped we would get chocolate in ours because that was something we could eat right away. Before I continue with the opening of the parcel, I have remembered a stop we had before crossing the Elbe, when we were herded into a field, no shelter of any kind, then it started to rain hard. Chaps gathered round the guards demanding shelter. It became threatening, so they got permission for us to shelter in the village church. We all trooped up and into this small church; space was soon taken up. Two chaps got up into the pulpit. I had a pew but would have been better lying down in the aisle. We had not washed for a fortnight, and our wet clothes were beginning to steam. That must have been a hell of a smell, plus the fact that chaps with dysentery were relieving themselves in the entrance because the guards would not let anyone out. When I awoke the next morning, the first thing I saw were two chaps having a good scratch in the pulpit with their coats draped around the sides. It must taken a good many weeks to have got rid of the stink.

So back to the opening of the parcel. we had not got it completely open, when a cry went up that aircraft flying overhead were coming down in a dive. They were either English or American dive bombers. In the first dive, they dropped a bomb and fired cannon shells, the instinct is to run, which I did out across this arable field, together with most of the party. On the second dive, they fired cannon shells, so we suffered eight attacks from the four aircraft, killing lots of men. Two chaps I knew very well came over to see how I was. I had some shrapnel in one hand, but not bleeding much. One of the chaps who came over was limping; he took his trousers down to see an unexploded shell which had travelled up under his skin almost to his groin. When I got back to where had left my beloved satchel, I found a hole through it, no sign of parcel or chap I was sharing with. I went to a dressing station where they were collecting the badly wounded. Polish women had appeared from nowhere.

My mate with the cannon shell near his groin told me after it had been taken out, that he stuffed a blanket up between his his legs hoping that might help if it went off. Two horses and carts picked up the wounded and started off across country to a small town which had cobbled streets. We were placed in a corridor with seats down one side. The airman who played football in Stalag Luft 1 and was called Twinkle Toes, was lying on the floor moaning and saying that he was dying. My hand stopped bleeding and at that moment I felt a bit of a fraud for being there, but of course it could so easily have become infected. After it was bandaged, was sent upstairs to a ward and shared a two-tiered bunk with a New Zealander who was also slightly wounded. We were the only two able to walk. I well remember being given a large bowl of macaroni.

The next day a German officer told us to follow him. We went outside the building to a door where an oldish woman, dressed in black, was waiting. We went inside to find several coffins and German soldiers lying dead. The woman took us to a coffin beside which lay Twinkle Toes. We lifted him in and put the lid on; there was also a Sergeant Brown who had died. We returned to the ward slightly shaken.

The next day we were again told to "Follow me". This time to a courtyard where a horse and cart lay stacked with several coffins. when we moved off across the uneven cobbles, I remembered being afraid that some would fall off, as they were not tied down. We reached the cemetery where they were unloaded. A German civilian was directing where each coffin should go. Unfortunately our two had to go up a slope, and it was a struggle for us; we were as weak as kittens. Then began the job of digging the graves. An odd shell would come screaming over; the ones you hear have already passed, it's the ones you don't hear that get you. The Guard said we were going back for something to eat. I sized it up in my mind and decided that I would not be coming back to dig graves.

Later, after eating some more macaroni, I looked around for somewhere to go. I found some stairs leading up to an uninhabited floor and found a row of toilets which made me think it was formerly a school. I went in one, sat down and went to sleep. It was dark when I woke up. I went down to the ward and no-one said where have you been?

That night, the shelling became heavy; those who could, went down into the cellar, nurses, German soldiers, myself and the New Zealander lay on the stone floor and went fast asleep. I was woken by a Welshman with a rifle over his shoulder, who said to me "Have a senior Service". I jumped up a free man after four years and eleven months. I went up into the ward where there were several soldiers highly amused at the state we were in, different uniforms,

34

etc. One asked how long I had been a POW; when i said five years he said he was still going to school then.

I went out the front to see the troops going by. A German woman, who was crying, came running by saying that Russki Kommt ambulances had arrived to take the wounded away. We came to the bridge which we had crossed some days before. It was now lying in the river, and the houses on the east bank were flattened. We crossed over in an amphibious tank, then on again to a large former German barrack block. Here we spoke to females from England for the first time in years. It seemed very strange. we stayed the night here, and travelled on to an airfield where we saw the first jet fighters. Later that day, we boarded a Dakota which had been adapted to carry stretchers. It was wonderful when we crossed the English coast and saw the green fields.

"Oh to be in England now that April's there"

We landed at a small airfield near Swindon, and sat down to egg and chips, then an R.A.F. Hospital, called Wroughton, where a nurse took our names and addresses to send to our parent by telegram. My mother later told me that the local postman had told the postmistress that he was going to be the one to deliver it, and that he did.

The very next day, back into the ambulances to travel up into the Birmingham area, to an R.A.F. hospital. The nursing sister ordered me to bed as she said the shrapnel would be taken out the next day. I did not get into bed, but went for a walk instead, out into the countryside. This I really enjoyed; not having been able to do this for a very long time. When I got back the sister was waiting. I received a dressing down which affected me not one little bit. I had no time for authority at that period of my life. I wish it had stayed with me.

We were issued with new uniforms. Then, given the all clear to go home, travelled to Paddington, then to Taunton, caught the bus to my home, fourteen miles away. My younger brother met me off the bus, my parents had arranged some decoration for my homecoming.

Very soon afterwards, I was demobbed, and received civilian clothes, suit, etc, and so ended my six years in the R.A.F, five of which had been spent behind barbed wire.

This brings me to the end of my story.

J.V. Foster

Service Number : 645044
POW Number : 89

John Victor Foster

(Jack)

29th January 1920 — 18th March 2011

Printed in Great Britain
by Amazon